Your Beer Playbook

D. Wayne Pursell

ISBN: 1456510452
ISBN-13: 9781456510459

TABLE OF CONTENTS

ABOUT THE AUTHOR

The author of this book, *Your Beer Playbook*, is D. W. Pursell. This individual is an experienced beer drinker. Wayne was a longtime resident of the State of Virginia, forty-plus years in Virginia Beach, now residing in Las Vegas, Nevada, and Neskowin, Oregon. After years of drinking beer, the author decided that the general public should be made aware of the benefits and rewards of drinking beer. Without beer, life would be almost meaningless or a constant struggle uphill. So many people don't realize how beer helps to solve problems, improve health and influence the growth of the economy. Beer is a big, positive surprise for individuals each day. The author knows that good times are promoted by beer drinking, and he wants to share and reflect on these times in his book. So, beer drinkers should finish a beer and start reading to learn the positive value of beer.

ACKNOWLEDGEMENTS

Big thanks, a round of applause, cheers and appreciation go out to members of my family—my wife, Eleanor, and our sons, Brian, Darius and Donnie—who supported me in my beer drinking days. They have always known my appreciation and respect for good beer times. Another group of beer supporters who rallied for the reward times were the POETS. This team would meet, especially on Fridays, to celebrate with numerous rounds of beer. Again, I give a big salute to my family and close friends for the good beer times and positive memories.

INTRODUCTION

SIMPLE INSTRUCTIONS: Buy a 12-pack of your favorite beer, chill it till it's extra cold and enjoy a series of beers while you read about the world's most important beverage. As a bonus, after every few chapters, you'll enjoy *A Reflection Moment*, a deeper thought for you to contemplate.

THE POWER OF POSITIVE DRINKING

Drinking beer can be a positive act. There are many positive benefits from drinking beer. To avoid kidney stones, beer works out the kidneys and keeps you healthy. Beer helps the heart and works against cancer. Beer makes the skin healthier. The list goes on. <u>Beer makes you feel good about yourself</u>. When you feel good about yourself, you have more confidence. With this increase in confidence, your skill level is better, problem solutions are more numerous and you feel more relaxed about things. Your positive drinking attitude is uplifting and permits you to enjoy things you are doing. So often, you look forward to doing something and you know a cold beer will top off the event—it just adds to the pleasure. Only those beer drinkers can enjoy the positive power of drinking beer. The amount of beer drinking is always limited to the location, event and standards by which you live. It's a lot of fun to drink and enjoy beer. It's not fun to get a DUI, hurt yourself, throw up, get a headache, hurt a person, fall down, break something or make yourself look like a fool. When beer is drunk in a positive manner, it makes you a winner. Drinking beer supports your health, builds confidence, relaxes tension, settles the nerves and always makes you a better player.

A REAL BEER DRINKER

A true beer drinker is one who wants to reap the power that positive drinking offers. That is the main reason for drinking beer. Enjoy the rewards. <u>Put beer first and start practicing drinking</u>. Look for the positive benefits of drinking beer. There are so many, and a real beer drinker does not want to miss any. Drinking for the good times is good because it's a reason for celebration. Reward thyself for the good times. You deserve to comp yourself with a beer of your choosing. Achieving a goal and surviving a challenge or contest means that you need a beer, or more. If you have been successful, then go to the Reward Center. The purpose, of course, is to have a beer. Think about the reasons that you deserve to drink beer. <u>It's really a measure of success</u>. You worked hard for that beer. Have one, a six-pack or more—whatever it takes to enjoy the power of positive drinking. Drinking beer gives you so much positive energy to enjoy life. Better health is a major goal, relaxing to enjoy the rewards of a long working day, to help meditate the challenges ahead and plot a game plan, to focus on the current issues and be objective on the situation and to feel good about yourself. <u>A winner realizes the strengths gained from positive beer drinking daily</u>.

Your Beer Playbook

D. Wayne Pursell

CHAPTER 1
WHEN TO DRINK

One might say, when <u>not</u> to drink! People should always drink when they want to. However, most people drink when there is an occasion. Example: The Super Bowl game. This is an event. So, a person would definitely drink at this event. To put it another way, a person would drink at a celebration. Example: A wedding would be a great reason to drink. Another time to drink is during a meal. Example: A birthday party would be a super time to drink. People associate drinking with relaxation time. Example: Drink after work at a local bar or after cutting grass, or when you are in the hammock relaxing. Another time to drink is on a road trip. Example: A group of five people are driving 1,000 miles to New Orleans to celebrate a big event. Then, the designated driver does his job while the passengers enjoy cold beer from a cooler. A lot of people go to a special bar often to celebrate happy hour—ice-cold beer at your favorite bar where you watch TV and snack on appetizers. It's very important to know when to drink, but it's also nice to know where to drink. Consider the following ideas on the subject of where to drink.

Your Beer
Playbook

Tops Off,
Bottoms Up!

CHAPTER 2
WHERE TO DRINK

Where a person decides to drink is very important. The location, place or site has a big influence on drinking. Visiting a theme park like Busch Gardens would mean that the drink of the day would be Budweiser. During the celebration of St. Patrick's Day, green bottled beer is popular at most bars, so enjoy Heineken. A fun time is Cinco de Mayo—a Mexican blow out time, so enjoy Corona! You often find yourself drinking at a fun site, a comfortable location or a bar with great service. Lots of times, it's important to drink to the day. Example: Bottoms up for 4th of July, down a six-pack for the birthday and tie one on when you win the lottery. So, celebration is like a reward time. You deserve a beer, so have one. After surviving a hard day of decisions, you are entitled to the taste of a cold, refreshing beer at the location of your choice. Visit your favorite bar, settle back in a La-Z-Boy chair, hang out in the hammock, find a seat at the sports area of a casino, put a 12-pack in a cooler for fishing, have a pitcher at the bowling alley, pour a cold beer in a glass before you throw darts and pop a top of your choice at the next wedding. Decide where you want to drink to celebrate an event, special occasion and good times, and enjoy the thrill of it all with the beer of your choice.

Your Beer Playbook

A Word to the Wise: Beer

CHAPTER 3
DRINKING TECHNIQUES AND STYLE

It is so important how a person drinks a beer. An ice-cold beer does not need a cover. Feel the icy bottle, twist the cap and drink the taste of desire. After finishing the beer, look at the empty bottle and recognize that a second beer is ready to enjoy. Repeating beers helps you to reach the desired level of satisfaction. The beer you choose to drink can be foreign or domestic. Most people select one or the other and don't switch during drinking time. The best beer comes in an ice-cold bottle or ice-cold can. Either container permits you to pour it in an ice-cold glass. Beer tastes better cold. Drinking beer can be enjoyed better with snacks or appetizers. If munchies are not available, resort to finding peanuts and crackers. Many drinkers enjoy bars that provide food to go with the beer. However, there are times that only beer is available. Often after work, a group gathers around a truck tailgate to enjoy a cold case of beer. No food is necessary. <u>The beer is a reward in itself</u>. Drinking after work is a form of celebration that is done every day, but especially on Fridays. <u>Good beer drinkers enjoy beer on those days that end with the letter "Y."</u> It's something they look forward to and deserve. Always drink for your health, for the good times and for fellowship celebrations. <u>Remember, to be a successful beer drinker, you must start practicing</u>!

Your Beer
Playbook

Beer Raises
the Bar

CHAPTER 4
THE COST OF BEER

The cost of beer is no object. It becomes no object when you are celebrating winning and enjoying the good times. If a person won the lottery, received an inheritance or hit the jackpot game, they would not consider the cost of a beer. To enjoy something that you want to drink is no problem. The cost of beer is very reasonable when you consider the many benefits gained from drinking. A cold bottle of beer may cost as little at $1. It may cost up to $7.50 per bottle. Depending on where and when you buy is most important. A supermarket six- to 12-pack is cheap. Ice it down and enjoy the rewards. A beer costs more on New Year's Eve, but the celebration time can be worth it. After all, beer is for the good times! Consider the rewards, benefits and satisfaction gained from drinking beer. It's almost endless. <u>Beer really is cost effective</u>. No liquid gives you more pleasure than beer. It can be consumed on any day that ends in the letter "Y." The old saying—you pay for what you get—certainly applies to beer. Once you have purchased a quality beer, the rewards and benefits are not too far behind. Looking forward to drinking a beer with the anticipation of great satisfaction is the only way it should be. The cost of beer is more than reasonable when considering the cost of medicine and pills. <u>Consider beer a prescription in your daily routine</u>. Remember—"Conserve water, drink beer."

Your Beer
Playbook

Time Out
for Beer

CHAPTER 5
BEER THINGS

Hey, you ought to "Beer Up" every day. Each day, the fun shirt you wear should symbolize the love for beer. Many T-shirts have logos, witty sayings or beer action configurations. Don't stop with the shirt—put on a beer hat. So far, you look good. A keychain is a good place to keep a beer opener. The opener can be plastic, metal or a combination of both. Sometimes, a cigarette lighter is shaped like a beer opener, or a belt buckle will do the job. Another popular product for beer use is the huggie for the can and the zipper coat for the bottle. Whatever you use, it identifies the love for beer. The more items and places that you associate with beer, the power of positive thinking will encourage you to develop beer products, inspire you to pick up the pace and reflect on the good times. Many people enjoy signature beer coolers, chairs, blankets, pennants and boxer shorts. To own these items often inspires a real beer drinker. Show your beer spirit! Be a team player and a productive beer drinker. After all, those people who "Beer Up" on a regular basis enjoy the good times more frequently. Beer things can be given as presents. Buy the domestic or foreign symbolic beer products that provide the greatest spirit of celebration. A beer tankard is always a winning gift. So, "Beer Up" often in celebration style with your own beer buttons and more!

Your Beer
Playbook

Beer:
A Necessary
Element

CHAPTER 6
THE REVELER DRINKS BEER

So often, a person thinks positively about things, and this attitude projects a power to deal with difficult situations. To generate this power of positive thinking, an individual is usually a regular beer drinker. When drinking beer on a regular basis, an individual establishes a plan to govern his actions and habits. A regular beer drinker enjoys not only the time period in which he drinks, but also the locations or conditions under which he consumes alcohol. The beer reveler drinks at his own pace and never pushes the consumption of beer. As the beer container becomes less full, the drinker's thinking process becomes more active and creative. A second round of beer accelerates the power of thinking positively. Problems and controversial issues can be solved and more solutions are conceived. During round three, when you hear the phrase "Bottoms up," it's a signal to display leadership qualities that are generated by the power of positive drinking. Don't just suggest a celebration event coming up, but remind others of how they can reward themselves and enjoy the good times. The fourth beer makes things really pick up a notch, and your creative thinking begins to show. Brilliant ideas, concepts, programs and solutions begin to spring forth during the fourth round of beer. The thinking process has sped up, and your creative menu leads to discussion. By the time beer number five is consumed, you feel that you really are on top of things. As you kick back, relax and unwind, you share your views on good times and celebration events. The last beer finishes off a six-pack, but not you! Beer number six goes down smooth and easy. It knocks off any remaining hard edges and completes the attitude adjustment process for developing the power of positive drinking.

Your Beer
Playbook

Beer:
There is
No Substitute

CHAPTER 7
ULTIMATUM–INCREASE THE GOOD TIMES!

Enjoy the good times more with a beer. Can you imagine people being denied beer when they want it? There are laws forbidding the selling of beer on Sundays before 1:00 P.M. Other laws make a county dry—no beer at all! Wanting a cold beer when you desire one is the ultimate need. You deserve a beer when you need one. <u>A cold beer stabilizes things back to normal conditions</u>. No beer could cause your life to be in shambles. So, think ahead, plan ahead and be ready to reward yourself at all times with a cold beer. Being able to enjoy a beer pulls the good times together and completes the circle for having fun. Let's have a beer— that's the signal to celebrate, enjoy yourself, have fun and to reward yourself for the good times. <u>Don't deny yourself the privilege of having a good time</u>. Other friends have fun, and you certainly need to be a part of the fun crowd. Don't put it off. Plan to have a beer celebration today. Without a beer, the celebration time can hardly commence. The beer signifies the good times have begun and serves as a reward well deserved. As an ultimatum to yourself today, celebrate the good times with a cold beer as a reward that you so richly deserve. Don't neglect other revelers that want to celebrate your good fortune. Even a small party would be in order, but a happy hour experience should be the minimum. The location to celebrate the good times is your choice. The ultimate decision to have a good time today is your idea, plan and reward. No hesitation is allowed—just do it! Remember, the attitude adjustment hour can always be extended to justify the satisfaction gained from a cold beer that stimulates the power of positive thinking.

A REFLECTION MOMENT...

BE YOUR OWN MAN

So, you've heard the expression, but do you know what it stands for? To be your own man, a male must be able to make a final decision, determine his true course of action and listen to other opinions. In addition, he must act on his own, maintain his freedom and independence, be his own master and stand up for his views and beliefs. Certainly, it would be nice to be your own man, but so many men are controlled by others— influenced by others or dominated by others. To avoid any of these positions, a male must learn early in life how important freedom can be to his status. It is never too late to be your own man, but you must be able to handle the responsibility. To be your own man, it is necessary to break away from controls, listen only to yourself, plan your course of action and show independence in his freedom of thought. Once a male has achieved the position, where he is his own man, then he can call the shots and resist outside influence. A male needs to practice his role to show his independence and freedom. First, he must plan his own goals, desires, time, celebrations and rewards. Enjoy his newfound freedom, independence and motivation excitement. A male who becomes his own man again is a freethinker, freedoer and free spirit. He is his own man to do, act and speak like he wants. The restraints are gone, the bonds are broken and a new direction is launched. Yes, you can be your own man—today and now!

CHAPTER 8
BEER IS THE REAL THING

Beer is the lifeline of the American economy. More beer is being consumed than ever before. People just love beer. Beer often serves as a reward symbol. Because so many people work hard, they deserve a reward. Therefore, the reward for excellent service is a cold beer. If a person works as hard as he thinks he does, then he deserves a beer every day that ends in the letter "Y." The cold beer symbolizes a reward for hard work. With more beer being consumed, more rewards are received and more work is accomplished. The success of the American economy is directly related to drinking beer, which is the catalyst to the power of positive thinking. The power of positive thinking is stimulated by the drinking of a cold beer. The absolute best thinking comes from beer drinking time. New thoughts are generated from beer drinking. New designs, creations, concepts and programs are all derived from drinking beer as a reward of success. To maintain that power of positive thinking that beer promotes, a person must be thinking "reward time" all day and night. Beer is a reward for the successful idea generated by drinking beer, which accelerated the power of positive thinking that conceived the original plan, which entitled you to have a cold beer and start the process again. Without cold beer, the economy would shut down and the power of positive thinking would be lost.

Your Beer Playbook

The Best Reward: Beer

CHAPTER 9
BEER—RANKS #1 LIQUID

Never lose sight of the benefits derived from drinking beer. It tastes delicious because you can choose the flavor. Some like a pilsner taste. Others prefer a bitter taste, like Beck's. It's your choice, and it all tastes great. Another benefit from drinking beer is crowd celebrations. If friends and acquaintances know that an event will be supplied with beer, then they will come. A big crowd permits easy networking, which leads to more business and profits. Any time you consume beer, it generates lots of rewards. Beer serves as a major source of energy. It makes you feel better and renews your youthfulness. It permits you to face challenges and win. It motivates you to do your best, and this means you don't give up or quit. A beer drinker demonstrates confidence, which brings out the best in him. As always, beer drinking brings the crowd together and generates laughter. Beer always lets you enjoy life and the spirit of freedom. When a beer drinker says, "Let the Good Times Roll," he is ready to celebrate and kick it up a notch. Don't put off the good times—no hesitation, just go for the gusto. Never put celebration on hold or consider doing it later. <u>Always uphold the high standards in drinking beer and reward thyself daily</u>. It's from this participation that the power of positive drinking is best reflected.

Your Beer
Playbook

The Solution:
Beer

Chapter 10
BEER IS A CURE

Nothing gives you more answers than beer. So often, an individual gets overburdened and needs to relax and unwind. This is a good time to drink beer. It would mellow out the individual and clear his head. As the beer drinker reaches round three, he is able to shrug off his burdensome problems by finding new solutions and answers to his situation. <u>Beer definitely helps to solve problems</u>. Beer actually provides answers. It stimulates the power in a person to think positively and generates multiple solutions. As more issues are resolved, the tension on the beer drinker wears off and he is ready to face new challenges with an attitude of positive thinking. <u>Beer always promotes the power of positive thinking</u>. This type of thinking is needed each day by so many worker bees who suffer from stressful situations. They seek prescriptions for relief and over-the-counter drugs. A sensible answer to bring fast relief from stress and headache situations is to drink beer. Give this individual a great location to drink beer, and his power of positive thinking will produce answers to burdensome issues, and the stress disappears almost instantly. Confidence returns and challenges can be conquered. Any beer drinker that receives credit for this newfound wisdom and creative solutions should acknowledge his source. <u>Always remember that beer is the answer to provide the solutions</u>. Enjoy the good times brought to you by beer and reap the rewards you deserve.

Your Beer
Playbook

Beer Can Help

Chapter 11
BEER IS 24-7

Sometimes, you might drink a beer at 7:00 A.M. and a friend might question your early morning thirst. Just say—somewhere it is 7:00 P.M., and I'm drinking on their timetable. Don't ever limit yourself to a beer-drinking schedule. Drink beer anytime and anywhere you want. Beer is always 24-7 in your own home. So, always keep a big supply at home for all celebration events. The refrigerator should be stocked with a minimum of a single 12-pack. Keep more beer in the pantry or garage for back-up. Emergencies often arise, and you need to calm the pace or energize the situation. When you need a beer is normally when you deserve one. So, reward yourself. Life is way too short to deprive yourself of the delicious taste of a cold beer. <u>Don't neglect your positive drinking needs</u>. It's always from those great drinking times that the most positive ideas emerge. For super ideas, concepts and formulas to spring forth, they must be nurtured by a moderated supply of cold beer. The profile that an individual sets from drinking beer demonstrates the power of positive drinking. <u>Remember that cold beer is the best remedy for all situations</u>. When a person is happy, more beer continues the jubilant feelings. However, if a person is down and out, a cold beer provides the answers and reassurances. <u>Obey your tastes and drink cold beer today</u>.

Your Beer
Playbook

Beer Has
No Limits

Chapter 12
BEER IS THE MENU

Beer signifies the good life. Enjoy the fruits of living and drink a beer! No way can a person enjoy a celebration without a beer. A beer sparks the excitement to celebrate. A beer initiates the celebration time to begin. Beer keeps the celebration flowing and motivates the revelers to pick it up a notch. Beer drinkers are very positive people who enjoy the good life. Beer alone can ignite a party in a positive direction. People get motivated when they drink beer, and the power of positive drinking accelerates. When a person enjoys the good life, beer definitely boosts the sounds of celebration. When good times are celebrated, beer is consumed as a reward for the event. Always remember, "Beer is the menu!" Nothing else is necessary. Ice cold beer is a menu by itself. One cold beer after another—it sparks a rally to continue the celebration and take it to a new level. Once you achieve this new level of success, the power of positive drinking also reaches a new level. It is beer alone that empowers this new level of positive drinking. Creative answers come more frequently, solutions are more abundant and leadership expressions are numerous. It is from this celebration mood that the beer drinker demonstrates his craft skills. He may demonstrate by throwing darts, playing cards or rolling dice. The power of positive drinking will direct him to victory. After all, the good life is generated by good beer. A beer drinker is always a winner, and his power of positive drinking is generated from ice-cold beer on the menu!

Your Beer
Playbook

Beer: That's
What it Takes

Chapter 13
BEER FIX

Have you had your beer fix today? Beer drinkers love to enjoy the first cold beer fix of each day. The beer fix is a signal to the body that more relief is on the way. Wow—what a pick-me-up! The cold beer seems to fix everything—a refreshing drink that satisfies the taste every time. <u>Don't neglect the beer fix</u>. After all, you deserve a cold beer reward. <u>The cold beer is a tribute to the success of the day</u>. A beer reward is deserved each day, and today is no exception. Ahhhh, the beer fix is on today. Pace yourself each day looking forward to the relaxing time with a cold beer. The fix gained from the beer is spectacular. A beer drinker gets so much from the cold liquid. For example: <u>Beer is a misunderstood vitamin</u>. As a person enjoys a cold beer, vitamins are added to his body system. A beer never drains a drinker. Instead, it pumps up the body systems to enjoy the good times. A beer fix should be administered when necessary. If an individual wants a cold beer to initiate the morning activities, then a beer fix is required. No time limit. Enjoy 24-7. Reward thyself when it is needed. Participation is the key factor for a beer fix to be successful. If you fail to reward yourself a beer fix, then you are not participating. Without participation, you cannot succeed. Good times are ahead, and each celebration signals the need for a beer fix.

Your Beer Playbook

Beer: A Liquid Capsule

Chapter 14
BEER REWARDS

Beer offers so many rewards! When an individual is successful, he or she deserves a reward. A cold beer is a reward well deserved. A person never gets tired of a cold beer. It settles the nerves and generates a new spirit at the same time. It's no big deal, but a cold beer at the right time is a satisfying reward. It tastes good and satisfies the needs. Beer rewards come frequently and for a variety of reasons. After an eight-hour workday, a person deserves a cold beer as a reward. Other reasons for having a beer include closing a real estate deal, buying a new vehicle, winning a sports bet, making a winning casino bet, relaxing after 18 holes and graduating with another degree. There is no master list for having a beer. The list of reasons is unlimited. Therefore, some people enjoy a beer for less complicated reasons. It's after work, so let's have a beer. There's football on TV, so get a beer! It's time to wash the car, while drinking a beer. There's a new beer, so let's have one. The painting job is done, and a cold beer sounds good. It's poker time, so get out the beer. The need for beer is unlimited. <u>Beer serves as a reward in so many situations</u>. Beer solves problems and generates so many new ideas and projects. The power of positive drinking is the beer reward so well deserved after a successful day. Reward thyself daily. <u>The ultimate reward is a cold beer</u>. Cheers all around for a cold beer to celebrate the good times!

Your Beer Playbook

It's All About Beer

A REFLECTION MOMENT...

REWARD YOURSELF...NOW OR LATER

What is it about a reward that we like so much? I'll tell you—it makes you feel good. A reward signals a need to celebrate. A reward symbolizes recognition for achievement. A reward calls for a photo session. A reward calls for planning. For example, if you won a trip, it would be a reward, and you would start planning. However, you may never win a trip, a prize, a contest or a drawing. So, how do you overcome this bad luck? Simple answer—you reward yourself now! Think about it—that's enough. You deserve a reward now! A reward means that lots of fun is ahead. You will have good times. You will enjoy yourself. So, ask yourself—Why should you reward yourself later and push the good times to a later date? By the time a later date arrives, the enthusiasm has dwindled and the anticipation has lost its glow. Your future is now! Your reward should be now! The good times are here for you now. Act now, and be a doer! Be positive about your reward. You deserve a reward. After all, you are a winner, and your reward is your desire. Consider the #1 reward that you deserve now. This will be your reward. Take the necessary steps to enjoy this reward now, not later. As a positive person, you do things in your life as quickly as possible. Get things done. Finish the job. Tackle new work and complete the task. Believe me, it's fun to reward yourself. And, to reward yourself now is the best thing to do. The bottom line answer is—It's better to enjoy your reward now than to lose, forget or change the reward! Just do it. Reward yourself!

Chapter 15
BEER GRAIL

It's never out of your reach. To enjoy your favorite beer without facing a dilemma is a real treat. Imagine that beer is not accessible! Horrible idea! Suppose no beer could be found. How bad would it be not to be able to quench your thirst with a beer? After work each day, you sought out the beer grail and failed. The beer grail was always illusive. Well, the good life is not like that at all! The beer grail is accessible after work or at any time you need the reward. The beer grail is the measure of good times and fun celebrations. <u>Hail to the beer grail!</u> It's always 5:00 P.M. somewhere, and it's time to drink beer. Clock time represents no restrictions. No holds barred on the beer grail! The beer grail signals "Let the good times roll," so pour the beer on time. The beer grail allows no restrictions, no limits and no hesitation. The symbol of the beer grail is recognized on both the local and worldwide levels. The beer grail brings excitement and serves the needs of many each day and night. The beer grail promotes the positive power of drinking and launches the celebration events to a new level. No blues, no headaches and no problems with the beer grail in action. The beer grail dominates the good times, fun times and all party times. <u>Think about it—it's already beer grail time.</u>

Your Beer
Playbook

Beer is the
Only Choice

Chapter 16
BEER MEANS NO BRAKES

Trying to make a decision should always be easy to do. So often, a person wants to do something, like buy an item, or go somewhere, and they can't because someone puts the brakes on the idea. When someone puts the brakes on good plans, the economy is set back, emotions are deflated and creative feelings are shot down. Brakes really halt too many things too often, too quickly, and create disaster. Maybe the idea of brakes should be abolished or restricted. If a person is around people who like to put brakes on aspects of society, policies of the economy or issues in politics, then that individual should consider seeking people who dislike using brake statements! Brake people can smooth out their negative thinking with a few cold beers. <u>Most people enjoy no limits to their freedom</u>. People enjoy good times without boundaries. Who needs brakes to slow them down? Beer means absolutely no brakes. People who slow things down or stop progress are breaking down society's growth. People who use the "no" word on a regular basis are resentful to new ideas and fast progress. A beer drinker is always supportive and shows creative ideas on new subjects. A beer drinker is willing to push things forward and is always willing to say "yes" to keep things going forward. <u>Life is too short to say "no."</u> Beer permits a person to think positively without hesitation. The power of positive drinking is always generated by consuming cold beer. Without beer, brakes would be put on thousands of ideas each day. However, since beer is available, good beer drinkers move plans forward, solve major problems and initiate the solutions necessary for growth in the 21st century!

Your Beer
Playbook

Best Beer:
The First

Chapter 17
NO WORKING DURING DRINKING HOURS

Perhaps the most famous quote used by beer drinkers. If you are having fun drinking beer and the times are good, then don't spoil it by starting to work. Working can be postponed and done later. Happy times and good moods don't come often; so, don't spoil the rhythm by working. Drinking schedules dominate, while working is secondary. A favorable drinking schedule is 24-7. Using this schedule eliminates all unpleasant work and complicated projects. Drinking beer time is important, and you don't want to lose the opportunity. Working can interfere with good beer drinking hours, so you set the golden rule. Just try saying it—Beer Time—and working halts. Open a cold beer as a reward, and relax. The drinking hours have begun and working is cancelled. While drinking beer, it's okay to play darts, shoot pool or pitch horseshoes, but no labor. Work is forbidden. Just like water and oil don't mix, neither do drinking and working. Think about it—every time a person is drinking and tries to incorporate some work project, he gets hurt. Harm comes to those who drink and try to work. Drinking hours are important to our health, and working during these hours can damage our health. Always be wise during drinking hours, and don't permit yourself to work. Maybe we should all have a work badge and wear it when we are not drinking. This type of identification may cause a labor stigma image and hostility. Workaholics can be a menace to our society, whereas a beer drinker promotes a positive image that sparks economic growth. Money spent during beer drinking hours trickles down to thousands of people and pumps up the economy. Increase your drinking hours and stop working.

Your Beer Playbook

Beer Says It All

Chapter 18
BEER WELL

A well is a source from which a person can get H_2O. This is a valuable resource to all individuals. It has become so important, that restrictions have been placed on its use. I would hate to see its use limited in the production of beer. Such a step would infringe on our beer rights. Conserve water, drink more beer. Go to the beer well more frequently. A refrigerator is the most popular beer well. It keeps beer cold and provides ice for the cooler. Another beer well source is a tavern or bar. Once again, the liquid gold is stored in a refrigerator. A favorite beer well is a cooler used at the beach, stadium, picnic or tailgate activities. No other source offers a variety of a single product enjoyed by so many people at celebration times. A sincere beer drinker keeps a mental list of beer wells. These locations provide the primary beverage that is needed at happy hour or reward times. A beer reward is always a priority goal and symbolizes success. So often, an individual will go to the beer well seeking a brewski that provides stability, settles him down and permits him to focus. Beer provides so much comfort in a short time. An individual should never deprive himself of a beer and its benefits. Beer rights cannot be jeopardized when beer products mean so much to our daily lives. Enjoy your beer rights daily. Never lose sight of the coming of beer restrictions and its negative impact on our drinking rights. Keep recycling the beer wells and support beer rights over H_2O rights any day!

Your Beer
Playbook

Beer Now,
Beer Later

Chapter 19
NATIONAL BEER DAY

How many days out of a year can a person name that celebrate an event or an individual? Yes, an individual can name quite a few. For example: Independence Day, July 4th, or people's rights exhibited by M. L. King. However, this nation does not celebrate a National Beer Day! Instead, we tend to celebrate with beer any weekday that ends with the word "day." Using such drinking time promotes congeniality and allows no excuse for missing celebration times. After work, an individual will celebrate the end of a workday with a cold beer. Wow, it would be fun to celebrate National Beer Day every day. In fact, there would be no date on the entire calendar more important than National Beer Day. Each day, an individual could look forward to rewarding themselves with a cold beer. However, this nation deserves a single day to be designated as National Beer Day. On such a day, beer banners would fly high, signs would be in windows, beer parades would be moving, beer songs would be played and celebration pictures would be taken. National Beer Day would certainly be exciting and a boost to the economy. Individuals would buy beer stocks and beer memorabilia, beer taverns would be packed and people would sport beer patches on their jackets. National Beer Day would always signify good times and be associated with celebration spirits. National Beer Day would symbolize a day to protect your right to beer. Each adult must protect his right to enjoy beer. On this day, each individual would protect his right to enjoy beer. On this day, each individual would protect his right to beer by buying and consuming the liquid gold of his choice. Remember, a National Beer Day would have a positive impact on this nation. A National Beer Day flag would be flown in each state capital to symbolize the greatest beer day of the entire year.

Your Beer
Playbook

It Starts and
Ends with Beer
Problems

Chapter 20
BEER PROBLEMS

Drinking beer is normally a happy experience, but beer problems can disrupt good times and cause frustration. Most beer drinkers try to avoid beer problems, but they will happen. A common beer problem is receiving a warm beer in a bar. Not so good. A buddy hands you a bottled beer—normally a twist cap—but there's no beer opener in sight. After a few guzzles of beer, you check out the beer date—UGH!—six months old. Then, most beer drinkers have suffered from running out of beer, hurt by a curfew, running into a dry county, visiting a place that doesn't carry your favorite beer, not having a beer huggy to hold the cold beer, missing a weekly sale on beer and ice melting too fast in the cooler. Many of these beer problems can be solved by practicing common sense solutions or smart beer drinking habits. People don't plan to fail, they just fail to plan. Always be a smart beer planner. Think ahead. Anticipate beer problems. For example, always carry a beer opener and drink at the same bar to enjoy your favorite product and service. As a smart beer drinker, you must plan for the future—buy two cases of beer! A beer drinker is a winner, and this coincidence is shown in his beer habits! Enjoy your favorite beer each day as a reward to your success. Always remember that beer promotes positive attitude solutions. By planning ahead, it gives the beer drinker the edge to be a winner. Remember, beer problems can be eliminated by a beer planner who is a winner with an edge to succeed.

Your Beer
Playbook

Beer Day—
Always Good!

Chapter 21
LIFE WITHOUT BEER

Such a situation would only mean that you were not having a good time. A true loyal beer drinker always prepares to have beer nearby at all times. Carry a cooler with a minimum amount to see you through the tough times. Always plan ahead to be able to buy beer or go to the beer cooler. Life without beer in unacceptable. Each individual must be able to get beer without hesitation. Again, it takes planning. Potential problems include curfew at nighttime, a dry county and beer looters! Access to bar, availability of beer and selection of beer should never be a problem. Every time a person maps out his or her daily plans, it should include calculations for beer recovery. For example: During an ordinary eight-hour workday, a worker bee would only down a single longneck for lunch. The daily planner would then focus on beer sources after work. It's always best to go to a favorite beer lounge directly after work. Nothing is worse than beer dehydration. To prevent this health condition, each individual should have a spider-designed network to retrieve beer immediately after work. Beer at this time is a necessity and lifesaver. Your body will respond positively from the liquid gold, and you will feel rejuvenated. Without beer, there would be no life. Each beer drinker looks forward to the cold beverage to stimulate and revive the exhausted body after work. A good beer habit provides a better lifestyle. An individual feels better when he can count on something each day, and beer is the one product that delivers that flavorful taste and spirit of new life. Pace your beer time, enjoy each bottle and drink beer for life. Life without beer should only happen when you are dead.

Your Beer
Playbook

Beer Generates
the Economy

A REFLECTION MOMENT...

PAST ← MEMORIES → FUTURE

Pop up a past memory! It may have happened yesterday or last year. Whatever—all past memories were good or bad. When we pull up past events, celebration meetings, trips or situations, we try to pull up the positive and good memories. It's fun to reminisce, but it's more exciting to envision the future. So often, we think about plans for the future. Example: We plan to go on a trip, so we envision stages of our trip, which will later become memories. So, the bottom line is this—If we want to have good memories, we must envision great plans around events, celebrations, trips and good times. It's time for you to single out one future memory moment and plan for its execution. It's time to preserve a future memory that you choose and plan. So often, this experience will be so important, that you will take pictures and have buddy proof of that memory time. Remember, the past has a place—museums, archives and old brain cells. It's the future planning for the good times, celebration events and buddy camaraderie that's really important. Don't dwell on the past; focus on the future. Work at living, not dying. You have been a part of the past; now plan to be a part of the future. This plan will be like a reward, which you deserve. Make your plan catch up with the future as your memories of the past will generate and stimulate more future memories that you envision.

Chapter 22
BEER HAS PERSONALITY

The way a beer tastes helps to determine its personality. A beer should leave a pleasant taste in your mouth. A taste that you enjoy and want repeated. An important part of the beer taste is a result of the chill on the beer. An ice-cold beer is always preferred. A frosted beer bottle picked from a bucket of ice helps to mold the personality of the beer. To enjoy such a beer when a person is steaming hot is a remarkable moment. It is also a time when the drinker bonds with the frigid beer and requests more. Remember to draw a smiley face on the frosted bottle. When you pour a beer, the foam rises on the top, and that is a sign of respect to the personality of the beer. As you pour a beer, the liquid gold sound signifies the great personality of the beer. Many beer buyers are influenced by advertisements that generate beer personality images. For example: Budweiser likes you to think that their product is the King of Beers. Sam Adams is "Always a good choice" and Miller Lite says, "Great taste, less filling." So many other beer producers try to influence your beer selection, but you know the real deal. The best beer is the next one. Enjoy the personality of each beer and the pleasure it brings. Sometimes, it's necessary to upgrade the personality of the beer you are drinking. If you need to spend more money for a better quality beer, then do it. Consider the beer purchase a reward that you certainly deserve. The new beer will lift your spirits, quench your thirst and step up your celebration time that you deserve as a reward.

Your Beer
Playbook

Focus on Beer

Chapter 23
BEER IS THE ANSWER

Sometimes, we face problems and issues that can't be solved or fixed. So, that is the time to have a beer. A cold beer settles you down and takes off the edge. This first beer calms you down and helps you to readjust your thinking. Don't push the panic button and formulate an early opinion. Rotate your thinking and look at your problem in reverse. Think out of the box. Now, have a second beer. Loosen up, relax and be flexible. This beer represents something good, and it's refreshing. Your spirits are higher and the power of positive drinking is now unleashing new ideas, plans and answers to deal with problems. Beer is the real deal. Your thirst is up for a third beer, so have another. This third beer is like adding premium fuel to your solution package. The problems you faced are smaller or gone. You can now really think about your needs—the first is to enjoy another beer. Settle back and think about your success. Since you are a successful person, you need to reward yourself. One more beer is ordered, and you deserve it! No hesitation is required. Why are there sometimes problems? Because people with problems don't have cold beer. Have you ever seen a person drinking their fifth beer, looking like they have problems? Answer: NO! No problems surface when you are drinking beer. Beer is the answer. The U.S.A. economy revolves around the mother lode—beer. Beer is the spark plug for success. The reward for success is always a cold beer. If you have a cold beer to spearhead the project, program or idea, and another as a reward for the solution, then you truly recognize that beer is the answer.

Your Beer
Playbook

All Solutions
Can Be Found
in Beer

Chapter 24
BEER DRINKERS IMAGE

If you want a beer, just order it! A loyal beer drinker enjoys his beer anywhere, and all the time. Beer drinkers are not influenced by the wine list, well drinks or mixed hybrids. A beer drinker just wants his brand—cold and served quickly. Drinking beer in public restaurants, bars and entertainment events is a standard image. Competition for beverages can be found, and beer lovers always win. A good example: <u>Nevada is for beer lovers</u>. This state has set the highest standard for drinking beer. In Las Vegas, a casino player gets complimentary beer for the asking. As long as an individual is a player, he gets served beer at no cost. This request can be domestic or foreign beer. Whatever you deserve, you get. When you leave a casino with a beer, it is no problem to walk with it on the public streets. Drinking beer symbolizes good times and celebration spirit. Beer can deliver the same punch as wine or hard liquor, it just takes more. There is never a need to drink beer fast, only at your own pace. Free beer offered to the player at casino games just makes it more enjoyable. Drinking beer in a casual manner is usually expressed just before winning a big hand or table stakes. After a beer drinker wins, a splurge at a casino bar is often witnessed. Beer drinking may go to another level and spark more excitement. Another round of good times; please excuse me, another round of cold beer. Whoopee!

Your Beer Playbook

Beer is Our Friend

Chapter 25
SOMEDAY

Our lives revolve around the calendar and each day of the week. We always plan to do a task, enjoy an event or take a mini-trip or vacation beginning on a certain day of the week. The days of the week are repeated on the calendar each month. For example: If we miss Monday Night Football, we will catch it next Monday night—no problem. We end a workweek usually on Friday with a happy hour gathering. Same deal—if we miss it, we catch it next Friday afternoon. It's the big desires we almost never do. We don't have the time—special events, celebrations, family meetings and big vacations are always put off. A popular excuse is that we don't have the money, time or family support, or there are other obligations. The most favorite answer for rejecting a commitment and avoiding a good times event is to say, "I'll do it someday." Of course, people want to do things when an invitation is given, but they often respond with the phrase, "But I will someday." The use of the word "someday" is really a false hope expression to cover up the lack of ability to do something now. So many people just can't do things for a variety of excuses. So, they explain their feelings by saying "someday." I will do it, go there, see it or enjoy it—someday. Well, you know what? <u>Someday is not found on any month of the calendar. Someday is not a day of the week.</u> Instead, it is an expression meaning that at some time or future date you plan to experience something you always wanted to do. So often, that time never comes. Sorry, you missed an opportunity earlier in your life. As life goes on, it gets harder to do things you could have done earlier. So, say good-bye to doing things you could have done earlier. So, say good-bye to someday and say hello to now. N—for next—choose a weekday, O-okay, I'll do it. W-Will bring what we need. Good times are for now.

Chapter 26
A MAN FOR ALL SEASONS

A season is a period of time. Each year, we enjoy the four weather seasons—summer, fall, winter and spring. Each season is different, but enjoyable. Another popular season is the hunting season. Individuals are allowed to hunt for a specific time period. The most popular season is the Christmas holiday season. Even though we have only one day designated as Christmas, we still enjoy the holiday season. This is a time to celebrate. Everybody enjoys celebrating Christmas day, but the holiday season offers so much more. It gives each individual the opportunity to celebrate every day before and after Christmas day. During good times, we need to enjoy ourselves and celebrate the holiday season. For many, the holiday season starts after Thanksgiving and goes until two days after New Year's night. A person should not lose sight of the numerous days for celebration. Never limit yourself just to celebrate the weekend days, but keep up the pace seven days a week. Credit yourself for each day of celebration. Never slack off; instead, reward yourself with another day of celebration. There is no excuse for not celebrating each day of the holiday season. If you miss a day of celebration, you cannot get it back—it is lost forever. However, if you plan better for the holiday seasons, you can get more celebration experience and achieve more rewards that you deserve. The four weather seasons cover the calendar for one year. For me, this is a logical plan to follow for celebration time. I do not want to lose the edge needed for celebration, so I see each day as a part of some holiday season. Each day represents an opportunity to celebrate the good times, and it's in my plan to enjoy them. Don't deny yourself the opportunity to enjoy the holiday season, which never slows down or ends. Celebrate the good times today because more are coming and you want to be a man for all seasons.

Your Beer
Playbook

Beer: So Much
More than Just a
Breakfast Drink

Chapter 27
HAVING FUN YET

What is the recommended allowance for having fun? No book gives the answer. Can one person alone determine the answer? Does a counselor or wife need to give a person the limit? When does fun begin and end?

For some, the recommended allowance for having fun is determined by money. The more money a person can spend, the more fun they can have. For others, it is determined by the number of vacation days a person is permitted to enjoy. Some people are only allowed a short period of time to drink after work and then go directly home. For a few, having fun is limited by work, duties, responsibilities, jobs, assignments, projects, debts, authority figures, time schedules and calendars. Many people cannot allow themselves to have fun until they retire or reach age 65.

Some people put restrictions on having fun and the allowance time is always short. Example: A person allows himself just enough money on Friday to have a single bottle of beer before going directly home after work. Cut it short—maybe 30 minutes of fun on Friday! With this type of restrictive thinking, a person is always in the box. They are always confined and limited. No room to move or expand.

There are other people who love to blow it out and have fun all the time. There are no limits on having fun. They have fun all the time. To have fun all the time, these people think that they deserve fun time. They consider fun times a reward for their hard work. They believe that the allowance for having fun is 24-7. No restrictions. Go for it. Just do it. No hesitation.

Every person needs to maximize his fun time—no boundaries or limits. Pick it up a notch—step it up! Be ready to have fun—say yes, let's go! Always allow yourself to enjoy the good times, reward yourself and celebrate all the events.

Your Beer
Playbook

Beer Allows
No Regimented
Schedule

Chapter 28
MAKE THINGS HAPPEN

Did you ever wonder why you didn't win the contest or win the bet? Have you ever been fishing and didn't catch a fish? Have you started a project and never finished it? THESE types of questions need to be answered if we are to succeed and move forward. To find an answer to these questions and other challenges, an individual needs to do one thing: Sit down and have a cold beer!

Have you had your first cold beer today? It will make things change. Enjoy a cold beer and change will come. In so many situations, you are faced with negative feelings, rejection, resentment and frustration. The possible reason for these complications is simple. You have not had your first beer of the day. Your first beer will always make a difference and provide a change. A cold beer helps you to relax and enjoy positive images. This first beer helps you to see things differently and in a positive way. A second and third round of beer generates new philosophies on subjects and stimulates new ideas to solve complex issues. As you settle down and relax, more of these things don't seem so bad, hard or difficult. As a matter of fact, after the fifth beer, an individual usually has reached a new level of priorities and the old situation doesn't need immediate attention.

To make things really happen, you need a supply of cold beer. Before you get ready to do a project, solve a puzzle diagram, confront a challenge or take on a task, you need to position your supply close by. Beer really can make a favorable change, put a spin on the situation and spark new ideas and direction. So, the next time things don't happen, pop open a beer and experience that upbeat feeling. For sure, good things will happen.

Your Beer
Playbook

Beer Helps You
to Take Steps

A REFLECTION MOMENT...

OLD MAN USED TO

So, you don't do as much as you used to! Maybe you have slowed down a notch or two. Perhaps you hesitate too much. Maybe you just lost interest. It could be that your energy level is low, or that you're tired or tuckered out. Your zip is gone, and what you used to do is now just too much to handle. You seem to be content with old memories and hesitate to accept challenges or preview a plan with five or more steps.

Your body and mind are in the idle mode. They need to be recharged, like a battery. Your mindset spark plugs need to be changed. That old slogan you said frequently—I used to do so and so—is now a lame excuse. Use your past experience to surge forward and plan ahead. Select your priority reward and prepare to achieve it. Make your five-point plan and fulfill each step. Example: Your goal is to attend the Super Bowl event in Las Vegas, Nevada, next year.

Step #1: Line up the time off surrounding your job, boss and customers.

Step #2: Lock in transportation and lodging.

Step #3: Start packing and secure all items for the trip.

Step #4: Set aside cash and extra financing.

Step #5: It is now your duty and responsibility to practice locally to experience what you will enjoy while in Las Vegas. Study the football teams to bet on, roll the dice for craps, buy football gear, work your camera, enjoy a football meal and drink a few cold beers. Get motivated. Nothing is difficult when you have a working plan, a new energy level, a get-it-done attitude and beer supporting buddies. Most of all, you'll discover that Old Man Used To is gone!

Chapter 29
SO, I DON T SEE IT LIKE THAT

So, I don't agree. The calendar says that Father's Day is only to be celebrated on one day of the year. Wow! What a break! Dads get one day off to have fun and be rewarded. Even then, it's limited. A celebration can be ruined by rain. One day isn't enough for a mini-vacation. Forget the one-day bit, and let the calendar read "Dad's Week!" That's right—a whole week to celebrate the good times for Dad. Every day that ends in the letter "Y" will be called Dad's Day. All dads deserve more than one day to celebrate. A week gives a Dad alternatives and room to adjust. He now has planning time and a window for a mini-vacation. During Dad's Week, he can rest, go to the movies, visit a bar, get a massage, go fishing, read a book, cook his favorite meal, play horseshoes, shoot pool, learn Texas Hold 'Em poker, take pictures or just rest in his Lay-Z-Boy rocker. Hey, whatever Dad feels like doing, he gets to make the call. It's his week to give the directions. Dad will make the decisions this week. However, seven days might be too much for the All American Dad. Remember, his decisions might blow out the weekly budget and upset the financial records.

With so much pressure on Dad to make fun decisions every day of a week could result in a disaster. Poor Dad could get stressed out, headaches, tired feet, aching back and high blood pressure. It even gets worse if he overshoots his credit card limit, his checking account and hits the red line. He begins to sweat. Fun times cost and rapid good times cost even more. Maybe Dad should slow down a bit. Peel back on the spending spree. Settle back on the fast pace. Stop trying to pick it up two notches. No more pep in the step. Relax—sit back. Nap time. Hey, you know maybe a single day called Dad's Day is just about right. Easy does it, Dad. You only really get your way 24 hours, once a year. That's all. No more. Same old, same old.

Your Beer
Playbook

So Many Choices
on Dad's Day

Chapter 30
BEER BLAMES AND SHIFTING

Oh, yeah. It's your fault it didn't get done. Well, if we had more beer, it would have been done on time. Beer must be present when a person is under pressure to get a job or task done. So many people fail to get a task done, so they blame it on beer—I didn't have any beer! Beer is a product that offers assistance in accomplishing so many jobs or tasks. A cold beer takes the edge off the challenge and lets the worker settle down to a calm pace to work. It's this relaxed mood that the worker performs at his or her best. Often a taskmaster will shift the blame on beer as a reason for a job not done or finishing a task. Never blame beer.

Beer creates smiley faces and promotes camaraderie. Beer is never at fault. However, in the midst of do-gooders, there are those that criticize and blame beer when production is slow and not finished. Beer generates the spark for work and motivates the worker. Workers know that when a job is done, more beer is getting cold as a reward. Beer drinkers know that beer is always a major part of production and should be present to generate support. Beer is a positive part of the solutions to problems. Beer gets its done and on time.

The cry "beer here" should be used by taskmasters when a project is underway. It's like a guarantee that the job will get done on time. As a final thought on working and drinking beer, the two go together. If people must work, they are entitled to drink beer. Workers can't complain about not having beer and employers can't shift the blame on beer if the job is not finished. It's this easy: Drink beer, work a little, reward yourself with a beer and show off your beer efforts.

Your Beer
Playbook

Schedule Work
Around Beer

Chapter 31
BEER PROBLEMS

Drinking beer is normally a happy experience, but beer problems can disrupt good times and cause frustration. Most beer drinkers try to avoid beer problems, but they inevitably happen. A common beer problem is receiving a warm beer in a bar. Not so good. A buddy hands you a bottled beer—normally a twist-top—no beer opener in sight. You check out the beer date after a few guzzles—uugh!—six months old! Then, most beer drinkers have suffered running out of ice, hurt by a curfew, drive into a dry county, visiting a place that doesn't carry your beer, having no beer huggie and running out of cold beer. Many of these beer problems can be solved by practicing common sense solutions or practicing smart beer drinking habits.

People don't plan to fail, they just fail to plan. So, always be a beer planner. Think ahead. Anticipate beer problems. For example, carry a beer opener or always drink at the same bar and you will know the product and service. Continue to be a smart beer drinker and plan for the future. Buy two cases of beer! A beer drinker is a winner, and this coincidence is shown is his beer habits. Enjoy your favorite beer each day as a reward to your success. Always remember beer promotes positive attitude solutions to plan ahead. Beer drinkers always plan ahead and this gives them the edge to be a winner. Remember, beer problems can be eliminated by a beer planner who is a winner with an edge to succeed.

Your Beer
Playbook

Plan Ahead for
Beer Rewards

Top Examples of Beer Problems:

- Hot beer at a restaurant or bar
- Expiration date on beer passed
- No glass offered by waitress
- Out of the brand of beer you want
- No beer plus munchies—free popcorn or peanuts
- Limit on variety
- No beer opener—no twist top
- Curfew on beer—time limit
- No ice for beer
- No huggie
- Dry county Sunday or permanent
- Bars promote drinking, but fail to help you get home—cab, rides, etc.
- Girlfriends failed to keep refrigerator full of beer—after all—it was the menu

Chapter 32
MY SPACE

Look around and answer this question: Do you have as much space in an area (that measures 5' X 10') that you can call your own? This space is absolute. Nobody can infringe upon this space. You control and dominate this space. You determine what goes in and out. You dictate what goes up near the ceilings and down near the floor. You can change colors of the wall, put more lighting in the area and change the floor from concrete to carpet. Go into this area and look around for possible changes. Feels good, doesn't it? So many men do not have an area or part of a room that they can lay claim to and determine what goes where and why. If a man does have a space, he can arrange how it looks, how things are placed and when there will be change. Then, this man has control over his own space and has a luxury in his own home. This space is normally not so big, certainly not 5' X 10'. However, anyone can take a small area and consider it a prize! A real treat! Control like this gives him more mental stability, flexibility and creativity. He has room to adjust, rearrange, shift and combine.

Having a space of his own, a man can plan ahead. He can put more order to his life and significant possessions. Those men that do not have a space of their own must share or do without. Some men are deprived of a space they can call their own. These men learn to do without and change their thinking on shared space. So often, these spaces get jammed with clutter and eventually he does not consider this space worth sharing. It becomes an area he visits less often, less frequently and less and less. So, how does a man get a space or an area to call his own? He gets lucky. He negotiates for it. He often settles for less. He re-thinks his choices. He does what he has to do. So, look at your precious independent space and rejoice. Celebrate with a beer. If it's not there or is cluttered, take some down time and have a cold beer anyway.

Your Beer
Playbook

Make Room for
the Big Dog

Chapter 33
REWARD YOURSELF NOW OR LATER

What is it about a reward that we like so much? It'll tell you. It makes you feel good. A reward signals a need to celebrate. A reward symbolizes recognition for achievement. A reward calls for a photo session. A reward calls for planning. For example, if you win a trip, it would be a reward, and you would need to start planning. However, you may never win a trip, a prize, a contest or a drawing. So, how do you overcome this bad luck? Simple answer: You reward yourself NOW! Think about it—that's enough.

You deserve a reward now! A reward means that lots of fun is ahead. You will have good times. You will enjoy yourself. So, ask yourself: Why should you reward yourself later and push the good times to a later date? By the time a later date arrives, the enthusiasm has dwindled and the anticipation has lost its glow. Your future is now! Your reward should be now! The good times are here for you now. Act now and be a doer! Be positive about your reward. You deserve a reward. After all, you are a winner and your reward is your desire. Consider the #1 reward that you deserve now. This will be your reward.

Take the necessary steps to enjoy this reward now, not later. As a positive person, you do things in your life as quickly as possible. Get things done. Finish the job. Tackle new work and complete the task. Believe me, it's fun to reward yourself. And to reward yourself now is the best thing to do. The bottom line answer is: It's better to enjoy your reward now than to lose, forget or change the reward! Just do it. Reward yourself!

My first reward will be a cold beer!

Your Beer
Playbook

Enjoy Your
Beer Now—It's
Necessary

Chapter 34
FIND SOMETHING TO DO

It's you, your girlfriend and her friend finishing an early dinner in a shopping mall, and a store catches their eyes. Situations similar to this happen often. Your better half will frequently say, "Let me look over there." You know what this message means to you—she is going to browse around. So, she wants you to wait. At this point, your built-in beer radar system turns on and the search begins. Sure, you'll wait—no problem. Give her space and time. Distance yourself. Find a new or old beer stool to rest on. Now, you can relax. No pressure, just sit back and plan for the weekend.

Being alone can sometimes be nice. It gives you an opportunity to open up a conversation with another beer drinker. New faces and new, shared ideas can only lead to bigger plans. Meanwhile, you should enjoy the munchies, TV, newspaper and napkins to write on. Your other half or girlfriend will dial you in with her trusty cell phone if she needs you or is ready to go. For the present, she has put you on pause like a DVD show. Yes, she will call when she is finished her shopping, so you should make the best of the unexpected free time.

Think about it—things are less complicated. If you were with her, she would expect your opinion on a purchase, and you can't win that one! She could ask you for advice—again, you will be wrong. So, you are the winner away from the browsing scene, sitting on a comfortable beer stool, enjoying your favorite cold beer.

Your Beer
Playbook

Tune Up Your
Beer Radar

Chapter 35
NEXT TIME

Why not this time? I want to think about it more; I am not ready to do it or prepared. I think it's too late to do it. Is there ever the perfect time to start a project, finish one or hang it up?

The next time I do something, I am going to do it right. Well, why not start right now? Take time out to have a cold beer. After all, it's 5:00 somewhere. The most important thing is that you have a cold beer on your time. It is not necessary to say I'll have a beer next time. Do it now. There is no hesitation, but a rational decision made by you. Why do some people wait until next time? Next time is later, and it may never come. Next time works for some postponers. People in doubt use the phrase "next time." Same deal for people out of cash. The positive person says, "Do it now," no waiting, get it done now. By doing it now, a person accepts responsibility and does not delay until next time. By having a cold beer when you want and need it represents a new attitude and not an excuse of next time.

Your Beer
Playbook

Begin Now, No
Hesitation

A REFLECTION MOMENT...

PRIORITY

Priority: Wow—what a word! We love to use this word, but we have lost the true value of its level of importance. So often, you use the word "like" to describe a feeling. It's so easy to say, "I like ice cream." The second level of value importance is "love." So often, you might say, "I love this movie." The third gesture of interest is "want." At some time, you have said, "I want that TV." The fourth word used to indicate a high level of desire is "need." This word is often used to describe condition. "I need a shot of penicillin." The fifth term used to describe a strong desire to fulfill a reward is "necessary." When something is necessary to achieve or obtain, it becomes a priority. For example: When an individual sees attending the Super Bowl celebration in Las Vegas as a priority goal in the coming year, then it is necessary to accomplish this challenge. Say out loud, "It is necessary that I go to the Super Bowl celebration in Las Vegas, and this is my most important priority above all others." The things you like, love, want and need are only of a short-term level of importance. Each of them only fills a brief level of satisfaction. They might contribute to your level of material gains, but they are short-lived and quickly forgotten. However, when you have worked, planned and achieved a priority, then you have accomplished a reward well deserved.

So, set your sights on the #1 priority that is necessary to achieve as a reward for yourself!

Chapter 36
LUCKY YOU

Words like these are not said often. However, there are occasions when they are said. When a person hits a jackpot, his friends would say, "Lucky you." Another time is when a person survives a wreck or accident. These words are said when a person meets and marries the perfect girl. These words are not used frequently because they explain rare situations. However, when a person says, "Lucky you," it means something special. Sometimes a person waits so long for luck to happen, and then it's just a smidgen.

So, how does a person become lucky frequently and often? That person might have the right horoscopes, carry a four-leaf clover, keep a special rock in his pocket, wear a special necklace, carry a special coin or prepare himself with something to bring him good luck. However, some people don't believe that objects or material things bring you luck. Luck just happens. Other people say you have to make your own luck. So, how do you make luck happen? To make luck, you must prepare for it. Example: If you go to a casino, you want to be a wise player, smart player, educated player and a professor of the game. When you possess these qualities, believe me...more luck will come. So, you need a gameplan, experience, confidence and determination. Luck can be all around you, so pull some your way. It is not always money that represents luck—it could be excellent health, a successful marriage, a profitable business and more. So, tomorrow, buy yourself a T-shirt that says "Lucky You" on the front, and wear it for your next big surprise. Love your life, and remember...your health is your wealth.

Your Beer
Playbook

Beer Can Make
It Happen

Chapter 37
SHOOT IT

A short phrase, but powerful words. These words are used in numerous places. For example, at hunting club events, at carnival contests and on aerosol cans to shoot ants. I use the term at craps tables. The person rolling the dice is called a shooter. So, the crowd often says, "Shoot it!" This means that the crowd wants the shooter to roll his point or an original number rolled the first time he threw the dice.

A lot of shooters drink beer at the table and usually swig some before rolling. A cold beer will mellow out the shooter and make him a winner. After setting his bottle down, the shooter will set the dice in a pattern to roll a number. He holds the dice between his thumb and middle finger. He lifts the dice and throws them down the table to a special spot. His entire movement is repetitious. No change between rolls. Lift up the beer bottle and enjoy the flavor of cold liquid. Position the dice and roll again. A good shooter will collect on each roll and drink beer every time.

Your Beer
Playbook

Be Quick—
Melt the Felt

Chapter 38
TIME OUT

Time out: This phrase means to take a break, rest awhile, and stop or halt. At any time during a day, an individual might take a time out. A task may be too difficult. A person may be exhausted. An injury may justify a time out. A person uses a time out to refocus or readjust his direction. A time out may justify the need for a cold beer. If a person is going to take a break, then a cold beer will help the situation and settle the nerves.

Even though a time out provides a break or rest, it's the beer that rejuvenates the spirit and sparks a new energy level. A person should never take more breaks than he has beer. The beer generates a new work level or production level. Every work manual, playbook or directions sheet should include a cover sheet with the words, "No beer, no work." It's a simple phrase, but immediately stimulates a workforce or individual enthusiasm. So, when individuals or members of a group take a time out, it not only provides a rest, but also a refreshment. Cold beer to the rescue, I say!

Your Beer Playbook

Break Time: Grab a Rescue Brew

Chapter 39
BENEFITS

When was the last time you enjoyed a benefit? Even more, did you deserve it? One type of benefit comes as a perk for an executive in a high-paying job. The benefit might be a new, bigger office, a personal secretary, a marked parking space or an extra week's vacation. No matter, benefits are good. However, most people do not enjoy big benefits with their job. In fact, most people don't expect benefits with their job because there are none. Example: A pizza deliverer provides his own car, insurance, fuel and maps. His only benefit is another delivery. A grocery store produce worker puts out fresh vegetables and doesn't expect any benefits—he just wants to keep working.

When you really think about it, most laborers and 8-5 workers don't receive any benefits. These hard working Americans often create their own benefits. Perhaps the favorite benefit after work every day is a cold beer. This special reward acts as an incentive to finish the day and enjoy another benefit. Benefits like beer can be enjoyed daily with friends, comrades, buddies or alone. Your daily success merits a benefit of your choice. Select a cold beer at your favorite bar and remind the bartender that it's a benefit from your job.

Your Beer
Playbook

Beer Can Be the
Best Benefit

Chapter 40
MINI-VACATIONS

It is these types of vacations that don't take much planning and they don't last long. For some, a mini-vacation may come at the end of a five-day workweek. It's Friday—lunchtime—and you decide on the spur of the moment to drive to the beach for two nights. So, you just do it. A mini-vacation is short in time, quick in planning and exciting to anticipate the fun! This type of vacation may require a short road trip. Experience kicks in the gameplan. Step number one: Buy a case of beer and ice. This one step covers at least 10 strategic areas of the mini-vacation:

First, the beer cuts the edge off the driving—it's for the passenger.

Second, it provides a pick-me-up once you arrive at your destination.

Third, the beer settles you down as you plan the nighttime activities.

Fourth, walking with a beer, if allowed, or having them in a backpack gives you a spark on your journey.

Fifth, the beer always serves as a reward and provides encouragement to make the next call.

Sixth, it's always fun to share beer with new friends.

Seventh, beer gatherings allow for making new plans and sharing new ideas.

Eighth, cold beer extends the night and delivers new motivation.

Ninth, when it's time to relax and settle down, it's nice to have a nightcap.

Tenth, calling it a night is well deserved—a short road trip and good beer times.

In review of a mini-vacation, there is one convincing item that accounts for its success—cold beer.

Your Beer
Playbook

Beer: The Main
Ingredient for a
Great Roadtrip

Chapter 41
IT COULD HAPPEN

So many times, a person thinks about a situation and responds with *it could happen*. An individual says *it could happen* as a possibility. *It could happen* means it might happen, or does it? So what. It's ridiculous to consider something could happen. Nobody controls the future. Anybody can make a correct, accurate guess or a prediction. But to say, for sure, that something specific will happen is ludicrous. People like to count on certain future situations. In fact, individuals plan on certain things to happen beyond the present. For example: Individuals make plans for the coming weekend because of certain circumstances. So, what could happen to spoil or change the plan? It could rain to spoil the outside event. People involved in the event could get sick. Yes, so many more dilemmas could ruin the weekend festivities.

If so many negative things could happen to destroy a planned weekend, how should a person move forward and maintain a positive attitude? The secret in being a positive person is to utilize the beer reward principle. Any time a negative feeling creeps in, a person should grab a beer and think positive. *It could happen* is never an option. Only the good survives. That's the way a positive beer drinker thinks. Beer drinkers are the true revelers—they live for the party. In fact, beer drinkers make positive things happen. There are no negative vibes from the minds of the beer drinker. So, when a party plan comes together, let the beer drinkers coordinate the situation!

Your Beer
Playbook

A Beer Reveler
Is Always
Shakin'

Chapter 42
SOMETHING NEW

We all like something new, or do we? Something new can replace something old. However, something new can represent an object or gift never owned. Something new can cost a lot or be relatively inexpensive. To say we all like to receive or buy something new is a true statement in most circles of friends. There are times when a person wants a repeat of an item or the same product. Example: When a person is consuming a Bud Light beer, he may not want to change or substitute when he reorders. His favorite beer is Bud Light, not Coors Light or Miller Lite. The beer drinker enjoys his Bud Light and something new is not wanted.

So, many times something new involves an increase in spending money. It may not be worth it. When is an increase in spending money for something new justified? Some of the following times or occasions may support spending more money for something new: Weddings, graduations, birthdays, anniversaries, Christmas and job changes. Something new is often received with a smile, a thank you and excitement to use it. Something new can also be too hard to assemble, not your color, not the right size or the wrong make. Something new should always represent an individual's best interest. If a person enjoys foreign beer, then don't present him an American beer or micro-beer. Give that beer drinker his favorite brand. Something new can be added to his favorite beer. It might include a bucket of beer in ice, a new beer huggie or his favorite beer memorabilia. Remember, something new is nice, but it can cause problems. If it does, then you already know the solution. Have a cold beer!

Your Beer
Playbook

Beer: The Multi-
Purpose
Solution

A REFLECTION MOMENT...

THERE IS NO FINISH LINE

This statement means that when you finish one task, another is waiting to be done. Or, when you finish one project, another is already set up to be done. Your work is never finished. You do some work and more work pops up to be done. You never finish your work because it never ends. How many times have you said, "When I finish this job, I will be through"? HA HA! Sorry, you are not finished—there's more work—maybe a time out, or pause or a shift in timetable, but the work schedule is endless. Sometimes, there is even more work to be done, more demands and more honey-do requests.

Since there is no finish line, how does a person cope with the endless work schedule? A person must reward himself. Examples: Often, a beer, a mini-vacation, a small party, a brief concert, a gift to himself, a short weekend camping, a picnic, a ball game, a movie or a family gathering. All of these are nice, but if you are married 15 years, these rewards become repetitious, doing the same thing, nothing ever changes and nothing is new. So, what to do?

Since there is no finish line, work projects never end and small rewards represent ditto relief, a person must seek a job reward that offers positive relief and reassurance that the future does hold a favorable timetable. So, what is the jolt a person should take to pick it up a notch and live again? The #1 relief valve and pick-me-up is a visit to Las Vegas. If you wait until you are age 80-100, forget it! If you are in your 70's, you will not ride the thrill-seeker coasters. If you are in your 60's, you had better hope you have none of the following problems to hamper your fun schedule:

NO: Hearing problems, sore muscles, eyesight problems, knee injuries, hip aches, neck problems, elbow difficulties, tired feet, spine aches or stomach weakness. These problems will slow you down from having fun.

So, just remember—there is no finish line, work projects never end, the same rewards get boring and if you wait too late in life to have fun, you will not have any fun. Plan to reward yourself big time before it's too late. Now is the time to enjoy life with a big reward for yourself. A reward for yourself includes your wife. Plan a trip for two to Las Vegas. Live a little now, so you can live a lot later, before Father Time and Mother Nature take their toll.

Chapter 43
HEALTH FIRST

Name something more important than your health. It's hard to do, or maybe impossible to do. Many people want more money first. More money will let you have a great time, but your health may suffer, and then what? Everything a person does affects his health. Example: He eats too much, he gets injured on the job, he gets hurt during combat duty, his safety lines break on the job, an avalanche covers him or he gets shot during a hunting expedition. So many jobs, vacation challenges, tours, motorcycle rides and bungee jumps can change a person's health.

To maintain good health, a person must become aware of potential problems that could change his health. With this knowledge, he could reduce the chance of injury. A dangerous situation is thin ice. If a person had to go out on ice and some of it was thin, then several precautions should be taken. First, have a friend to watch your path on the ice and distance from shore. Make certain somebody knows where you are and that if you don't call soon, you may need help. You can take a rope and attach it to something to pull you out of the water, if necessary. Adventures like this require extra clothes, perhaps a fire and maybe a boat. Getting out on thin ice could jeopardize your health permanently, so think ahead of the pros and cons. Because a situation like this is so dangerous and risky, a person needs a reward if the roundtrip is made safely. Settle back and enjoy a cold beer.

A cold beer will settle the nerves and relax the tension. The best thing about a cold beer is its value to good health. A cold beer is absolutely a plus toward good health. The benefits of cold beer are endless. Most beer drinkers know that it provides support to a male's plumbing system. It stimulates new ideas in open discussions. It generates positive action without hesitation. Finally, it stimulates an attitude adjustment toward feeling good.

Remember: If your health comes first, a cold beer helps to deliver that condition.

Your Beer
Playbook

B-6: Vitamin or
Six-Pack?

Chapter 44
··· AND THEN THERE WERE TREASURES

When I was walking on the ocean beach, along the edge of the water, I found a piece of washed glass. It was beautiful. The shape, color, size and weight made it a perfect collection item. I considered it a treasure.

Again, when I was hiking a trail in the mountains, I crossed a stream and noticed a unique rock in the mud. After picking it up and washing it off, I was amazed at its different colors and strata lines. I considered it a treasure.

I enjoy taking pictures. One time, I took a photo of the sunset west of the Pacific coastline in North America. A combination of the sun setting, the clouds opening up and the sky color made this picture a winner. It was so beautiful; I considered it a treasure.

It is a pleasure to relax in a green grass yard in a hammock. I did this one time in my back yard, and watched the wind bend over the grass. One time, as the grass parted, I could see a four-leaf clover. I got out of my hammock and plucked the biggest and prettiest four-leaf clover I have ever found. To me, it was truly a treasure.

A while back, I heard a political speaker comment on the unity found in the American society. In his speech, a phrase stuck with me. As a part of a quote, he said, "Together is a great place to be." I took these seven words and used them on a wooden plaque that hangs on my wall. I consider these seven words to be a treasure for directing my life and well-being.

Your Beer
Playbook

Each Day
Provides Its
Own Gifts

My concluding thoughts on finding treasures are brief. Many of the things that you consider treasures are personal and stay with you, usually a long time. Your treasures do not always cost a lot of money, but they can. Some treasures can be passed on to relatives or friends. An important quality of a treasure is the happiness it brings to your heart and memories reflected in its age. I have one final remark about my most important or my most prized treasure—I found it—my wife—on Marshall Street.

Chapter 45
LEARN TO COPE

Certainly, you want things to go smoothly and fall in line as you expect. However, it doesn't work like that. Problems come up, setbacks occur and no options are left. Buddy, you just need to learn to cope with the situation. You just got a new hand, so make the best of it. For example, a bill payment is late and a penalty is incurred. Well, pay it. Bite the bullet. Just do it. Get it done, and feel a sense of relief. The problem is now solved, and you deserve a reward. Relax a bit. Unwind. Calm down. Settle down. It's 5 o'clock somewhere, so have a cold beer.

Life if filled with ups and downs. Everything changes and ends. If you just ended something, it's time to start over. Celebrate like a band is playing your songs. Order another cold beer, and put some mustard on your pretzels. When things don't go according to your plan, develop a new one. People don't plan to fail, they just fail to plan. With a new plan, you now have a new direction, a new goal and a new attitude. Things will get better, and you are in control. You know that life is not always fair, but you don't leave the game. Take a break. Catch your breath. Relax and have another cold beer.

Your ability to cope with new situations, problems, issues and difficulties will improve. You can call the shots, make the decisions and turn things around in your favor. The important thing is to move on, without hesitation, and act in a positive manner. A positive attitude gives you confidence to cope with good times and bad times. So, celebrate often during the good times and reward yourself frequently. If you need to cope with a new situation, you have the skills to do it. Life can be good. Now is the time to celebrate the good life!

Your Beer
Playbook

Life Provides
Ups and Downs

Chapter 46
CHEAP BEER

Words of Wisdom: *"If cheap beer cannot*
save the economy, nothing will."

CHEAP BEER: 10 REASONS THIS IS A TRUE STATEMENT

1. Beer serves as a reward! The masses need this beverage at a cheap cost.

2. Beer helps to solve problems, complications and difficult situations. The more cheap beer a person drinks, an attitude adjustment will occur and numerous solutions will be offered.

3. No other products affect so many areas of the economy in a positive way. Beer promotes jobs—manufacturing, pubs and grills, grocery stores, ball games and events. When people buy beer, everybody benefits.

4. Save water, buy beer! This is true, and again, the economy benefits. Don't waste water, buy beer!

5. The economy needs a National Beer Day. More money would be spent on beer and more people would be happy.

6. Beer is like a medicine. It keeps the plumbing lubricated. It prevents kidney stones. More beer consumed makes you happy and may act as a sedative to make you sleep.

7. Consider the number of jobs created at each of the following events, and then consider beer as the major beverage: Weddings, anniversaries, graduations, business conferences, sports events and vacation cruises.

8. More stores need to market beer: Drug stores, grocery stores, gas stations, movies, mall booths and tour guides.

Your Beer Playbook

Save the Economy: Drink Beer

9. Beer sales would increase if the product were offered in more places: Summer beaches, water tours, local sports events and home delivery (like Pizza Hut®). The beer would give each person a boost to accomplish more and be productive.

10. Beer is also a survival product. Without beer, a person cannot survive. Beer is the nectar for great health and well-being. Beer provides the gusto feeling to be successful and get the job done. By buying beer, the economy will feel the jumpstart. More people will work and more celebration will be renewed.

Chapter 47
MAKE-UP DAY

There are over 50 days on the calendar that represent celebration, recognition or holidays. There are very important days for various groups, people, organizations and clubs. However, there is no date on the calendar that serves as a make-up day. During any year, a person may forget a birthday, fail to meet a person on time, miss a concert or simply make a mistake. Suppose the calendar had one day a year that allows a person to make up for his errors. Wow!

An opportunity to turn things around. An attempt to make things better. To improve on a past situation, a person may apologize, send flowers, purchase a gift card, offer a dinner date or meet for a new night out. The list is endless on ways to try to make up and apologize for a past mistake. I have found that one of the best ways to make amends, apologize, correct a mistake and to show sincere regret is to offer the second party a cold beer. Wow!

Yes, a cold beer offered to someone as a make-up day indicates that a sincere effort is being made to improve on a past situation. Don't stop there. The first cold beer was just an introduction to allow you to explain away the past problem. Settle down in a comfortable atmosphere and enjoy a few more beers. The cold beer will help. Smooth over the past issue or situation, allowing you to readjust your relationship to a new friendship level. Cold beer brings people together and allows for bonding. So, if it's a make-up day for you, please do it with a cold beer in a bar with the date on a balloon.

Your Beer
Playbook

Beer is an
Apology

Chapter 48
HIGH HOPES

We all get 'em. Sometimes it's when we want to win a lottery or we want great weather on a vacation. We can get our hopes high on just about anything we want to enjoy. However, so many times, our high hopes are dashed and a feeling of regret sets in. We feel like we are back to square one, or we scale back to our old ways of negative thinking.

Yes, high hopes make a person more positive, cheerful, energetic and excited. However, to fulfill these high hopes, a lot has to happen. I have found that a person needs a lot of luck to succeed in achieving these high hopes. A person makes plans involving high hopes, but in most situations, he has no control of the outcome. Don't make your hopes too high or unrealistic—they may never happen. On the other hand, people should not make low hopes. Yes, we all make hope statements every day, but few of them are high hopes.

I have found that a situation involving high hopes often calls for a beer. This liquid gold can settle you down before the end result. A cold beer can relax a person in an unpredictable situation and actually settle his nerves. If the high hopes are fulfilled, then the celebration begins. The cold beer now has a new meaning and status. Beer can take a winning situation to a whole new level. Whoopee—yahoo—carry on! Every once in a while, high hopes are fulfilled and dreams come true. When they do come through, remember what it took to achieve this wish because it may never happen again. Good luck, and have a cold beer.

Your Beer
Playbook

Dreams Come
True with High
Hopes and Beer

Chapter 49
PUZZLE

This is a word that can be used in a variety of ways. It could mean a cardboard puzzle you put together on a flat surface. It could apply to a scavenger game in which you must decide the best method to collect your list items. A person's disposition or a personality change can often puzzle a friend. For many people the art of living is a puzzle. Some never figure it out, others catch on a little and a few think they have a solution. For me, the art-of-living puzzle can be summarized in ten parts:

1 **Exercise**—Stretch, use weights. Build strength, set goals.

2 **Walking**—Get up and go. Get a routine. Use comfortable shoes. Build stamina. Jog later.

3 **Sleep**—Get it when you need it. Get enough.

4 **Eating**—Your waist should be smaller than your chest. Diet, if necessary. Chew your food carefully; choking can kill you.

5 **Vitamins**—Use a multi-vitamin. Learn the importance of each ingredient, vitamin, herb or item. Supplements help to strengthen the immune system.

6 **Projects**—Hobbies are examples. Plan a task. Set up a challenge. Example: Make a walking stick.

7 **Celebrations**—Reward yourself. Make celebrations frequent. They can be small, big, brief or elaborate. They can be for yourself, friends or relatives.

8 **Learning**—Read more. Learn something: Study a new talent, or earn a certificate. Learning increases your ability to achieve.

9 **Friends**—You need to be selective, but not rigid. They can help, be resourceful, share, be fun, be cooperative and be supportive.

Your Beer
Playbook

Take the Puzzle
Out of Life—
Have a Beer!

10 Challenges—They make you smarter. They make you think, work and become satisfied. They can make you feel like a winner. They can show your weaknesses and strengths. They can be fun and provide learning.

When I practice doing these ten lifelines, I feel good and carry on with a positive attitude. Maybe you see different answers to the art-of-living puzzle. That's okay! All of us have an art-of-living puzzle that needs to be solved.

A REFLECTION MOMENT...

THE COST OF FREEDOM IS INDEPENDENCE

A person must be independent to keep his freedom. Without independence, a person cannot be free. To be independent, a person must be free to make his own choices. A person cannot enjoy his freedom if he is not independent.

Independence was the cornerstone of the Declaration of Independence. A person must be independent to enjoy his freedom. Once a person has achieved his freedom, after gaining his independence, he can make his own decisions and choices.

Among the many freedoms that an individual enjoys is the right to make his own decisions and choices. These freedoms cannot be enjoyed unless he is independent. So, what must a person be independent of before he can enjoy his freedom? A person must be independent of controls. If a person has controls over him, then he is not independent to enjoy his freedoms.

What types of controls limit a person's independence and therefore restrict his freedoms? If a person is in prison, he has controls over him. If he commits to marriage, he has obligated himself to have controls placed on him. These controls can sometimes damage his independence and limit his freedoms.

If a person wants to enjoy his freedom, he must be independent from controls. Enjoy your independence and express your freedoms.

Chapter 50
WHILE IT LASTED

Nothing lasts forever. However, some things do last a long time. Those things we like that do last a long time often need repair and upkeep. A good example would be the old homestead. A very good car or truck might also fall into that category. Since most things that are important won't last forever, we need to enjoy them while they last. Perhaps a visit from a relative or friend is enjoyable, but it won't last for long.

With so many things bringing us happiness, excitement, pleasure, fun and entertainment, we need to capture its value to our lives while it lasts. One of the best ways to capture and lock in the memory of those good times is to take pictures. Participation in celebration events like the Mardi Gras needs to be captured with pictures. These photos can be enjoyed for years. Remember the last time you said, "I enjoyed it while it lasted." Okay, protect these magic moments, good feelings and happy thoughts with camera action.

If you look hard at these pleasant experiences, you will probably find that a cold beer was present. Even a cold beer doesn't last long, but it adds so much to the good times. You can always buy another beer, but the good times move on to another day and time. Capture the special times, people and events while they last. However, the taste of a cold beer can be repeated frequently to generate memories of the past and conversations of the good times. So, have a cold beer and good times all around.

Your Beer
Playbook

Beer: An
Experience
in Itself

Chapter 51
THINK AHEAD

Somebody is doing it, are you? For many, thinking about the present is usually enough to do. However, I sometimes think about the past, but I can't change any of it. Of course, that leaves the future. To think ahead, it leads to planning.

To make the best plans and cultivate creative ideas, you need a cold beer. A cold beer will really generate fresh ideas and motivate action planning. It's fun to plan ahead if you can expect to carry out the plans. Build on the future. It motivates you to be creative and enjoy your rewards. Thinking ahead can be done at any time of any day of the week and in any location. Some people think ahead in a group of workers. The group generates ideas and plans. Other people go to a certain favorite place to think ahead and plan.

For many, it's better to think ahead at any given opportunity. This means taking notes, jotting down ideas, reviewing materials on the subject and scoping out the ideas. If you enjoy thinking ahead, it could be costly. It takes time away from finishing present projects. Often a plan for the future is outlined and you realize you can't afford it and it's not realistic. This condition leads to frustration and discouragement.

To settle down and overcome this mental condition, you need a cold beer. Remember, a cold beer can act as a stabilizer and often renews favorable thoughts. Enjoy several beers and think about how you became successful and accomplished so much. It was probably cold beer that accounts for these victories and favorite memories.

Your Beer
Playbook

Future Ideas
Come with
a Beer

Chapter 52
NOT SO LONG AGO

Remember when things were going your way? Perhaps you had most everything worked out and no headaches. The time was when you experienced little problems, but certainly no big problems. Well, times have changed.

The ladder of success has doubled in length and the end is out of sight. The ladder of failure dominates the economy. Making ends meet is tough enough. Hanging on and keeping in there is a blessing. Everything goes into the checking account, then out. No savings exist—nothing there. So, what is the solution or remedy for the tough times? Well, there is no magic answer—no quick fix. Most people just need to stay afloat, keep their head above water.

When seeking answers to multiple problems, a person needs to first relax. Relax and ponder with an ice cold beer. A cold beer settles the nerves and calms the present state of mind. A cold beer actually puts you in control of your thoughts, answers and future planning. Drinking a cold beer says that you are happy for the moment and thankful for the cheer in your heart.

Your Beer
Playbook

Beer Here!
A Cheer to
Remember...

Chapter 53
REVIEW THE GOOD TIMES

When was the last time you said, "Let the good times roll"? Even if it was yesterday or a year ago, it's time to RENEW! All of the fun you had during the good times should be repeated frequently. It might be on a smaller scale, but it would signify the importance of gaining a positive attitude, planning for the future and anticipating the experiences the good times offer. Get that feeling to let the good times roll, and grab a cold beer. A cold beer will definitely stimulate the planning, setting goals and reflecting on the past good time experiences.

Even though the calendar shows numerous dates for celebration times like July 4th, birthdays, anniversaries and Valentine's Day, it's time to make room for renewed good time experiences. You might need to see a concert, see a fireworks display, rent a Harley motorcycle for the day or take a walk in the park. Keep moving and exercise. Generate new ideas and challenges.

What can you do to renew the good times before the fixed events on the calendar get you motivated? A cold beer will spark the positive ideas and good time experiences. So, have a cold beer and let the good times roll!

Your Beer
Playbook

Beer Motivates
the Good Times

Chapter 54
COLLECT–SAVE–HOARD

At some point in the lives of many people, this combination could become a problem. We all tend to collect something in our lifetimes. It might be comic books, sports hero cards or CDs. Whatever you collect, you need space to store it or secure it. After ten years, this collection of items could become a problem. Everybody saves things because they want to enjoy them at a later date. We all save photos to remind us of the past, a special setting or an event. Whatever you save, you need a place to put it. Some people save coins, and they need to be put in a special place.

In addition to collecting and saving items of personal interest, many people hoard things. They tend to stock up on things they might need at a later date. They could hoard grocery items, Christmas ornaments and clothing items bought on sale. When it comes down to the way many people live, it involves all three habits. The more a person does these three habits, the more storage space is needed. It might be a problem for some people to determine which of the three habits is most important. To solve this problem after 25 years or more, you need to let go of some of the items. Usually a person can sell some valuable items, give them to family members or make a gift of some.

Would you rather have a beer? Decisions, decisions—yes, I would rather have a beer. A cold beer definitely helps to solve problems and make smart decisions. When a person has collected, saved and hoarded too much, they deserve a cold beer to relax, mellow out and develop new directions to solve the situation.

Your Beer
Playbook

Too Much of
Something Can
Be a Good Thing

Chapter 55
WING IT!

So many times, we are given directions on how to do something. These directions are too often confusing, small print, no diagrams and no telephone number for assistance. No problem—*just wing it!* Use the engineering stamina beer provides, and just do it. Begin doing something and everything will fall into place. No hesitation, just do it. There is no wrong way on this job, just shift gears and on to the next step. After your goal is in sight, take a break. Enjoy a cold brew. Relax. Sit back and get some photo action shots of the project's status. Scenes like these are good memorabilia images. Have another cold beer—you deserve it.

As you continue to master this task, you might consider the finished product as a symbol of success or even representation of your flagship skills. Once again, you have achieved an impossible task or at least one that sparked the need for a cold beer as your guaranteed progress in completing your task. When this job is finished, there will always be another. No task is too difficult for you since you employ the confidence of *just wing it* philosophy. Around the world, the bright CEO will often use this philosophy.

Just remember that you can use the concept—*just wing it*—on all levels of leadership and apply it to any problem, job, task, situation and difficulty! How hard can it be? *Just wing it!* Use your imagination, improvise, exchange, blend, utilize and pursue. By using your *just wing it* skills, there are no limits on your success. As you conquer more challenges, your wing it skills will increase and you will seek more rewards. The cold beer will continue to spark your wing it skills and always jumpstart any task or assignment.

Oops! Another job—time to have a cold beer.

Your Beer
Playbook

What's Your
Beer
Philosophy?

A REFLECTION MOMENT...

LIFE IS GOOD TODAY

What makes life good today? Perhaps a lot of things, but one stands out as a daily supplement to make you feel better about things, especially your life! Have a cold beer.

A cold beer to me says it all. Pop off the bottle top and down a few gulps. Relax, stretch, roll your neck, breathe deeply and grab the beer for another swallow. So, why does beer make life good today? Five things come to mind. I can count on it to signify the end of the daily work schedule, I can count on it to settle me down to relax, I can expect it to generate new ideas and plans for tomorrow, I can enjoy this time because I survived the day and all its challenges, and the beer serves as a reward, and last, this beer is always so good, it calls for another round. Beer makes life good today, tomorrow and for all times.

A FINAL RECOMMENDATION

Get another beer...

Made in the USA
Lexington, KY
04 September 2011